HOW TO
DRAW
WITHOUT
eraser

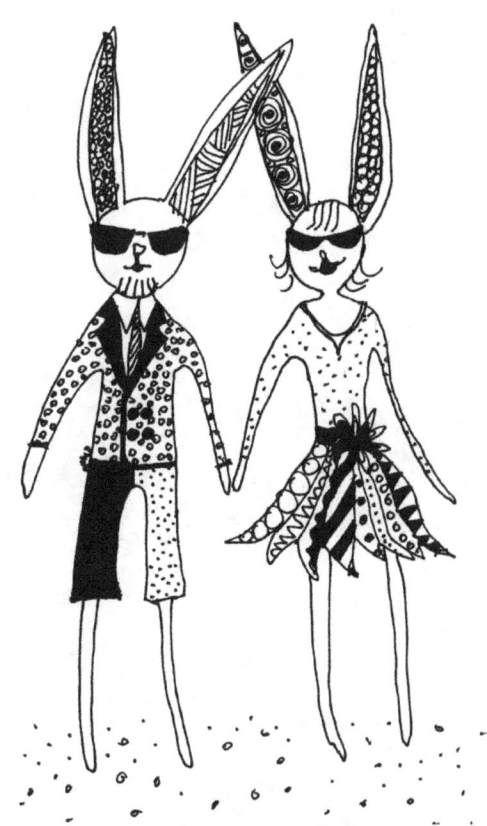

CHILDREN'S GUIDE TO THE WORLD OF

NeoPopRealism

NeoPopRealism PRESS
NADIA RUSS

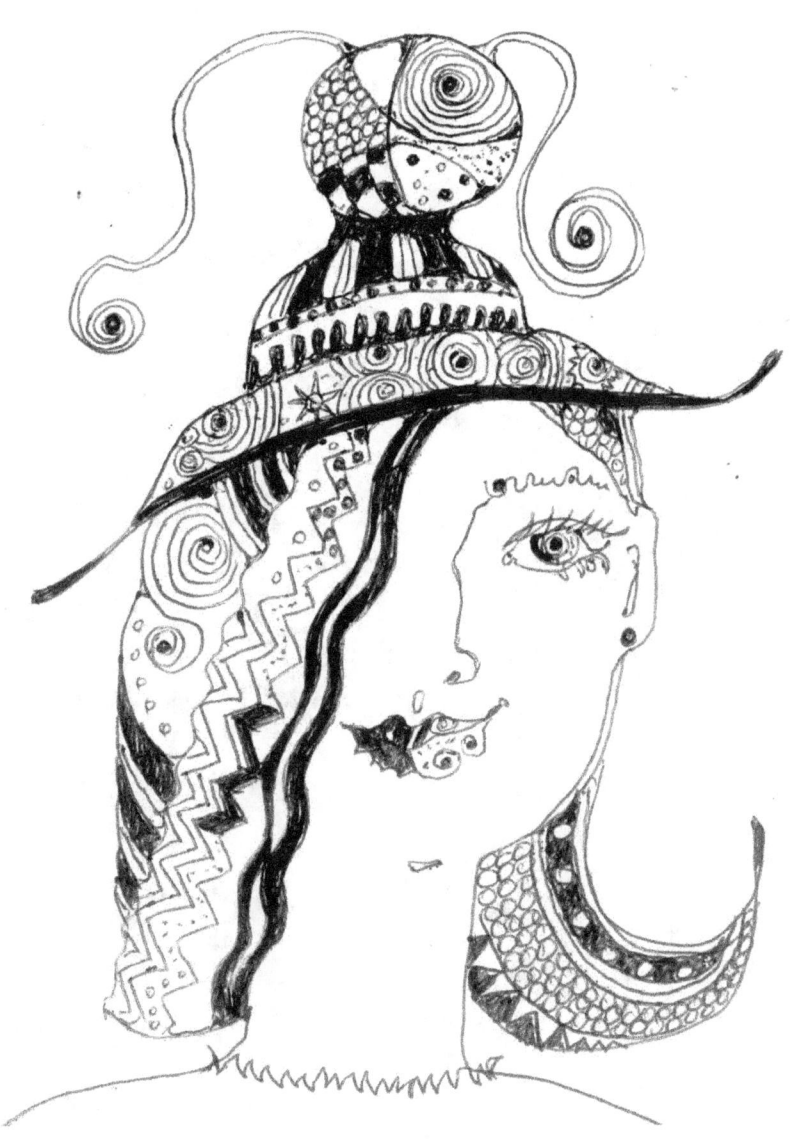

This girl is Nadia Russ' assistant, and she will guide you through pages of this book, Her name is Neo (aka New).

HOW TO
DRAW
WITHOUT
ERASER

CHILDREN'S GUIDE TO THE WORLD OF
NeoPopRealism

NADIA RUSS

NeoPopRealism PRESS

First time published in 2011 by NeoPopRealism PRESS
PO BOX 366
New York, NY 10013

NeoPopRealismPRESS@mail.com

How to Draw Without Eraser: Children's Guide to the World of NeoPopRealism

ISBN-13: 9780615521824
ISBN-10: 0615521827

11 12 13 14 15   10 9 8 7 6 5 4 3 2 1

Published in the United States
Language: English

This book teaches children how to draw whimsical NeoPopRealism ink drawings.

Author: NeoPopRealism PRESS
Images by Nadia Russ

www.neopoprealism.org

CONTENT

Introduction

*N*eoPopRealism ink drawing style (learn how to pronounce it correctly: *Neo-Pop-Realism*) was created by *Nadia Russ* in 1989.

Nadia loves to experiment. Why? Because experiment is always adventure! You should love experiment too. Today, you will find out how to draw with ink pen hedgehog, bear and rabbit. You will learn how to do it without eraser.

You will use the same, but simplified, method of the drawing as *Nadia Russ* used first time 22 years ago, when she created this art style. Then, *Nadia Russ* imagined that her consciousness left her body and flew to the Space. Why she did it? She loved an idea of being united with the Universe. *Nadia Russ* thought it will help her create something new, like no human being created before.

Then, when her consciousness was in Space, her body was in her apartment in Moscow. While her consciousness was in Space, Nadia Russ' hand created the line, which was flowing freely. Then, appeared sections her hand filled with the repetitive patterns - circles, triangles, squares, rectangles, dots, zigzags and their variations.

At that moment, *Universe* used *Nadia Russ* as a *Conductor* to create the absolutely amazing artwork.

Nadia didn't use eraser, because if a 'mistake' made, the following patterns balance the whole composition. Her drawing was unique; no artist did anything like this before. Later, she also began painting with acrylic on canvas, using the same concept.

January 4, 2003, in the United States, *Nadia Russ* created a word *NeoPopRealism* and internationally announced new style of visual arts.

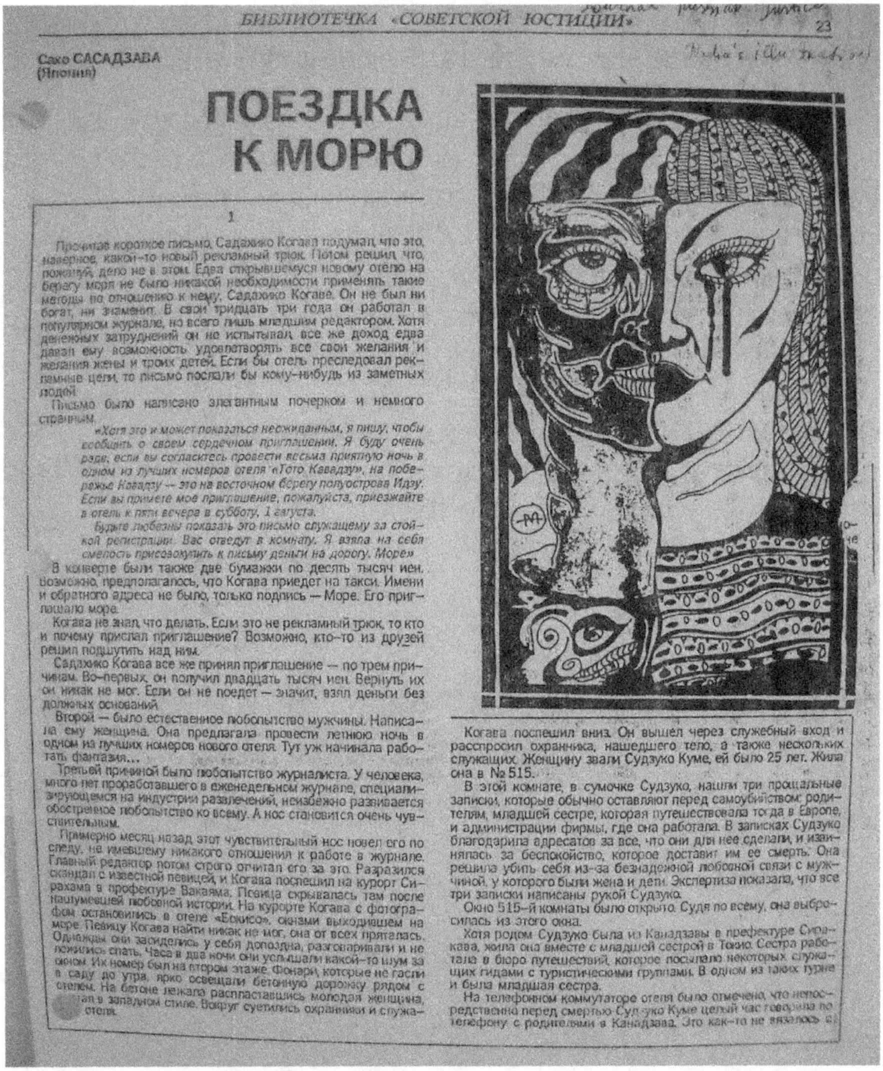

This is one of Nadia Russ' first ink drawings. It was published in *"Russian Justice"* Journal in Moscow, in 1992

TOOLS

Now, when you know what NeoPopRealism art is, learn about the tools. It won't be complicated. All you need is black ink pen *Foray Rolle Rollerball Medium 0.7 mm* or any similar. It can be thinner or thicker pen, all depend on what you would like to draw. Also you need a piece of cardstock paper 8.5"x11" or any other size or type of paper. Again, all depend on what you want to achieve and what is purpose for your drawing. Pen and paper can be purchased in Office Depot stores or in any convenience store locally.

We offer you to start drawing here, on special blank pages 31-42 of this book. Simply follow the instructions. Also, you can try to finish each incomplete drawing you will find in this book.

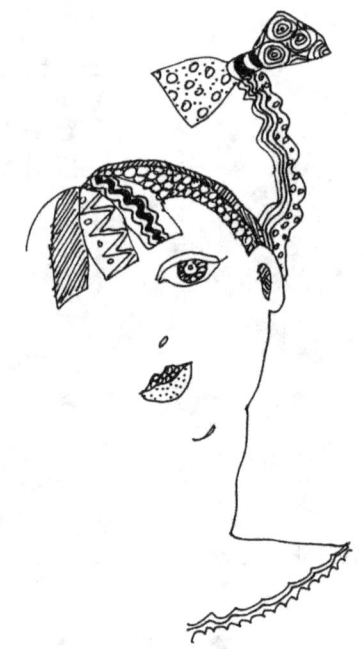

How to Draw a
HEDGEHOG

Let's start your exiting journey to the world of NeoPopRealism with drawing a hedgehog.

What do you know about hedgehog? Hedgehog has friendly, curious and humorous nature and adorable face. The quills cover his back. His little tummy is extremely soft and is covered with short hair. Hedgehog has a quiet, gentle disposition that makes him a true delight. Each has a distinct personality.

The following pages will show you step-by-step how to draw with ink pen a hedgehog. Every following image includes new details. And remember: no eraser is needed. The complete image will look like this:

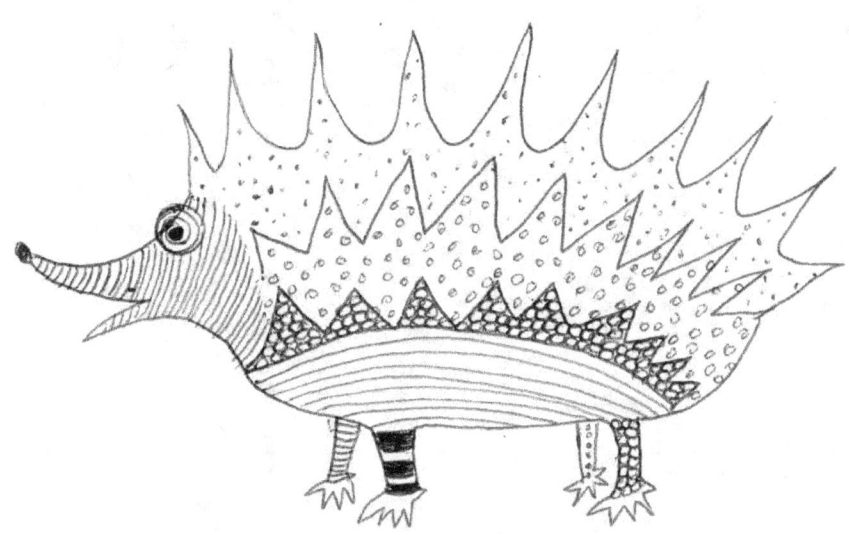

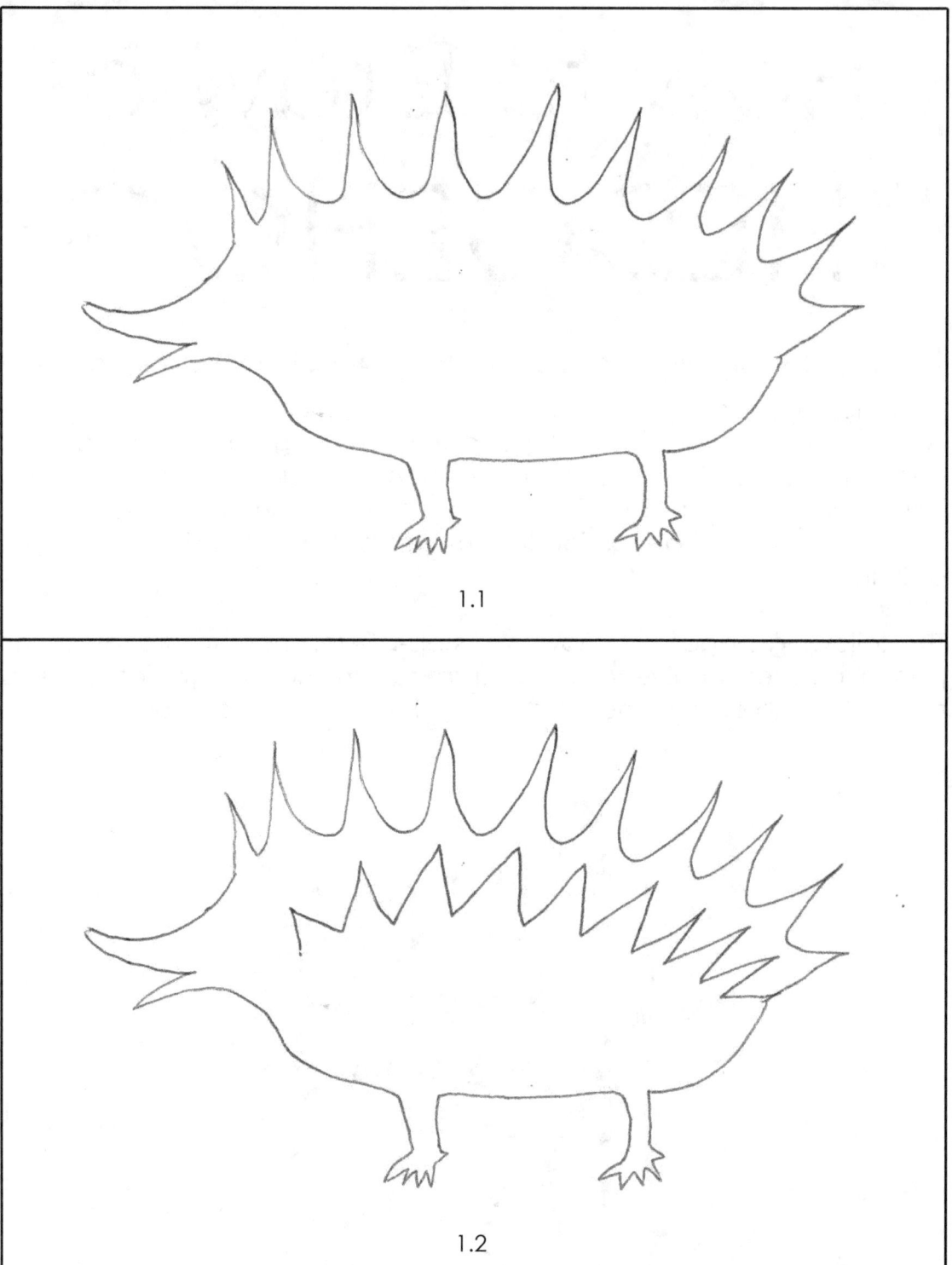

1.1

1.2

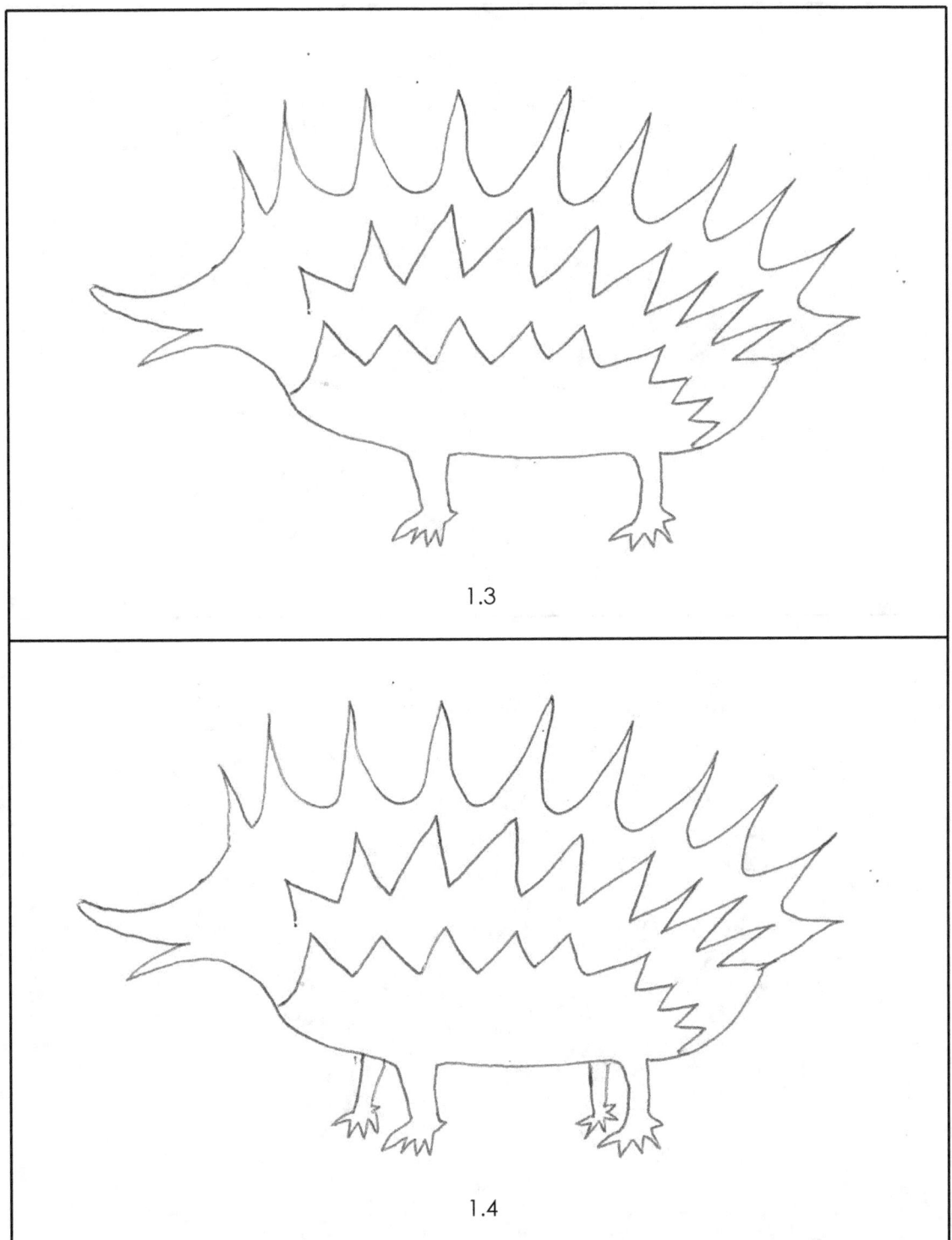

1.3

1.4

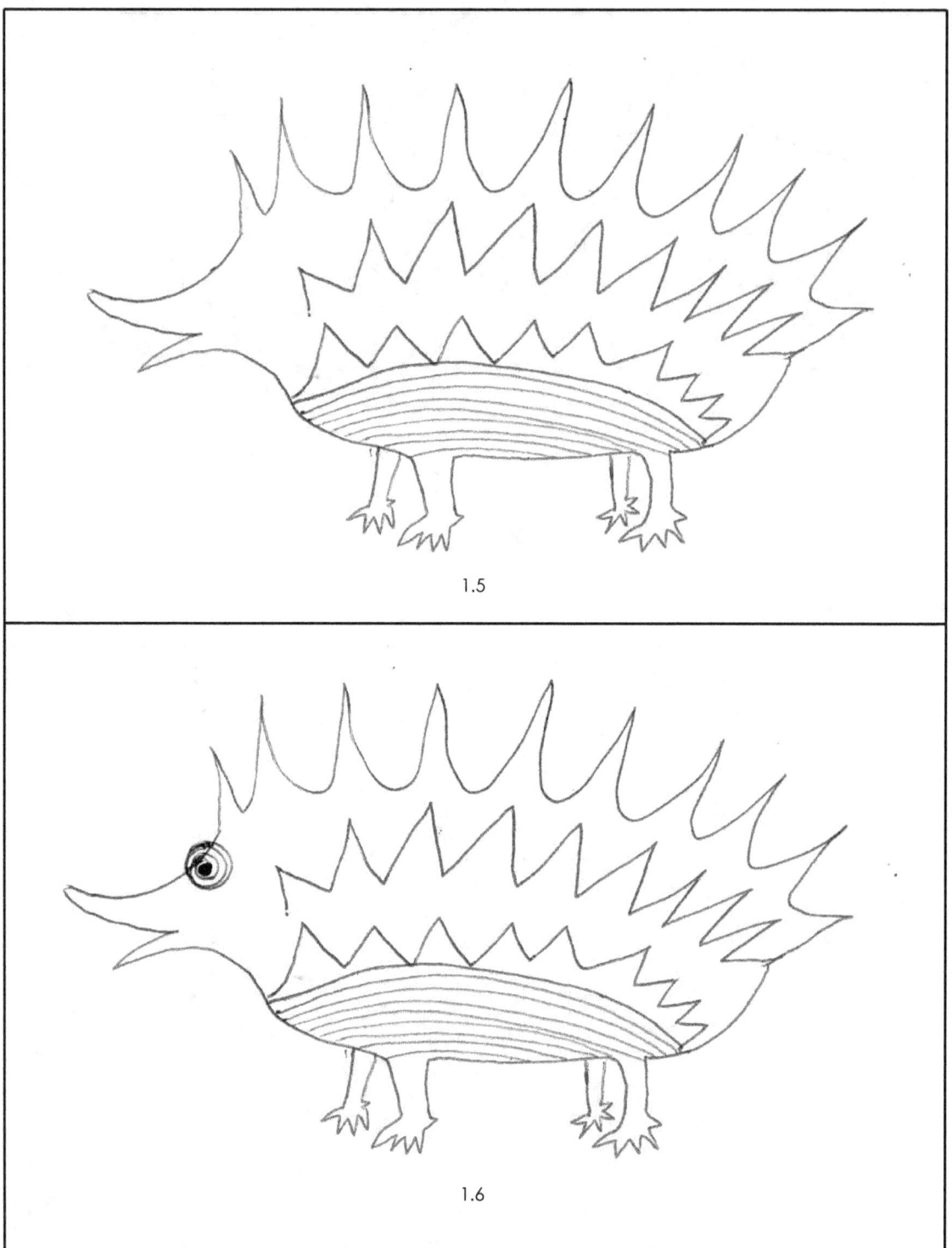

1.5

1.6

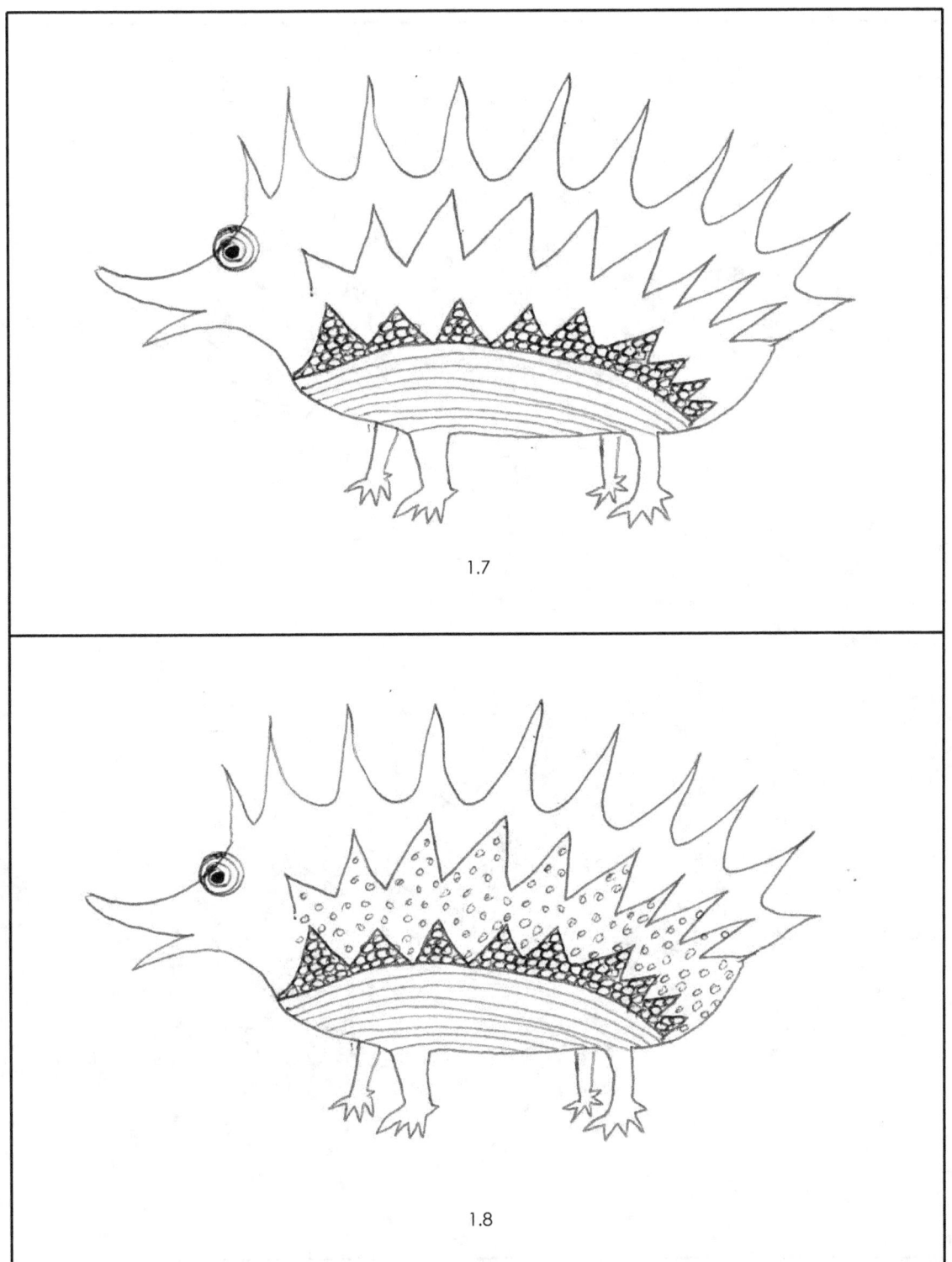

1.7

1.8

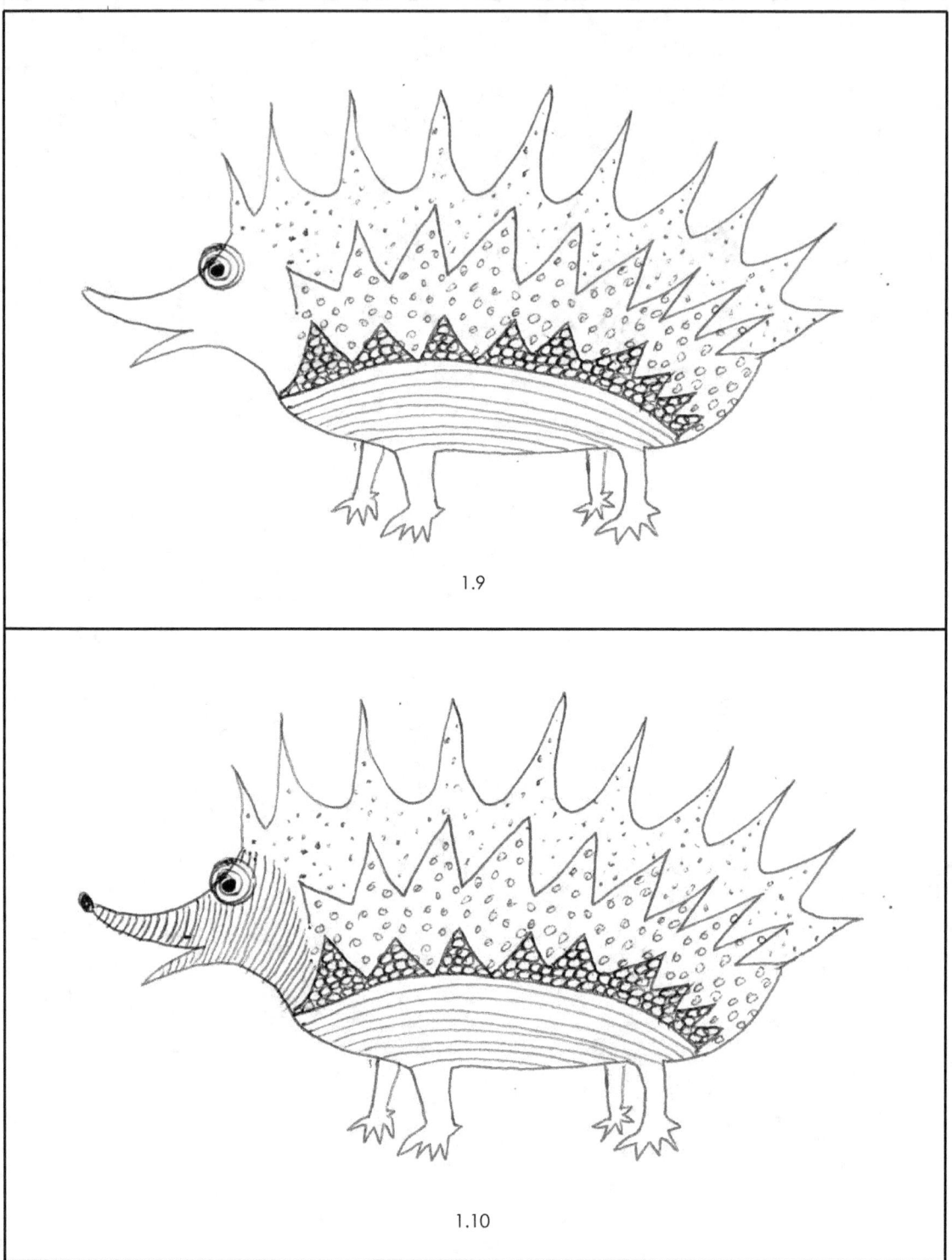

1.9

1.10

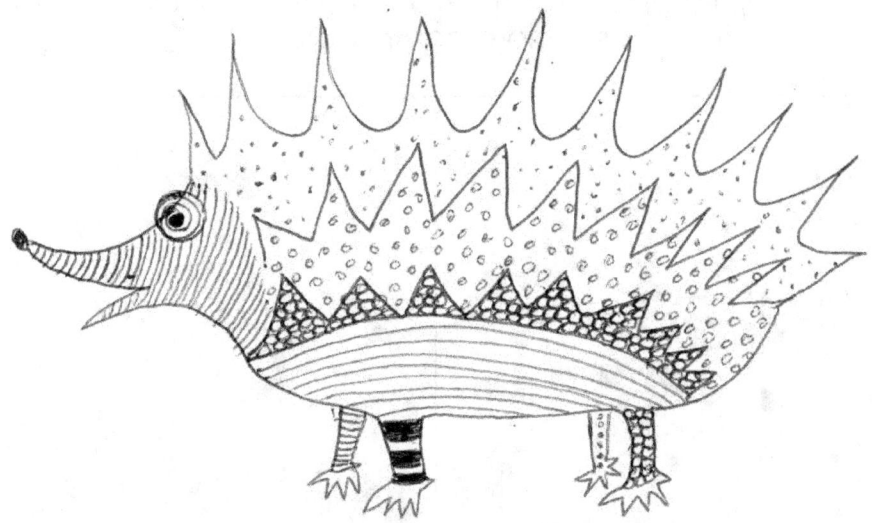

The Hedgehog

The following pages show you how to draw repetitive patterns, used in drawing "Hedgehog."

Sections, created by lines, you fill with different repetitive patterns. You can create these patterns using your imagination. These patterns can include the dots, circles O, squares ◘, triangles △, zigzags, and their combinations in any variations. But now, you will learn the very simple patterns. Later, after you learn how to draw the simple patterns, you will be able to create those, more complicated.

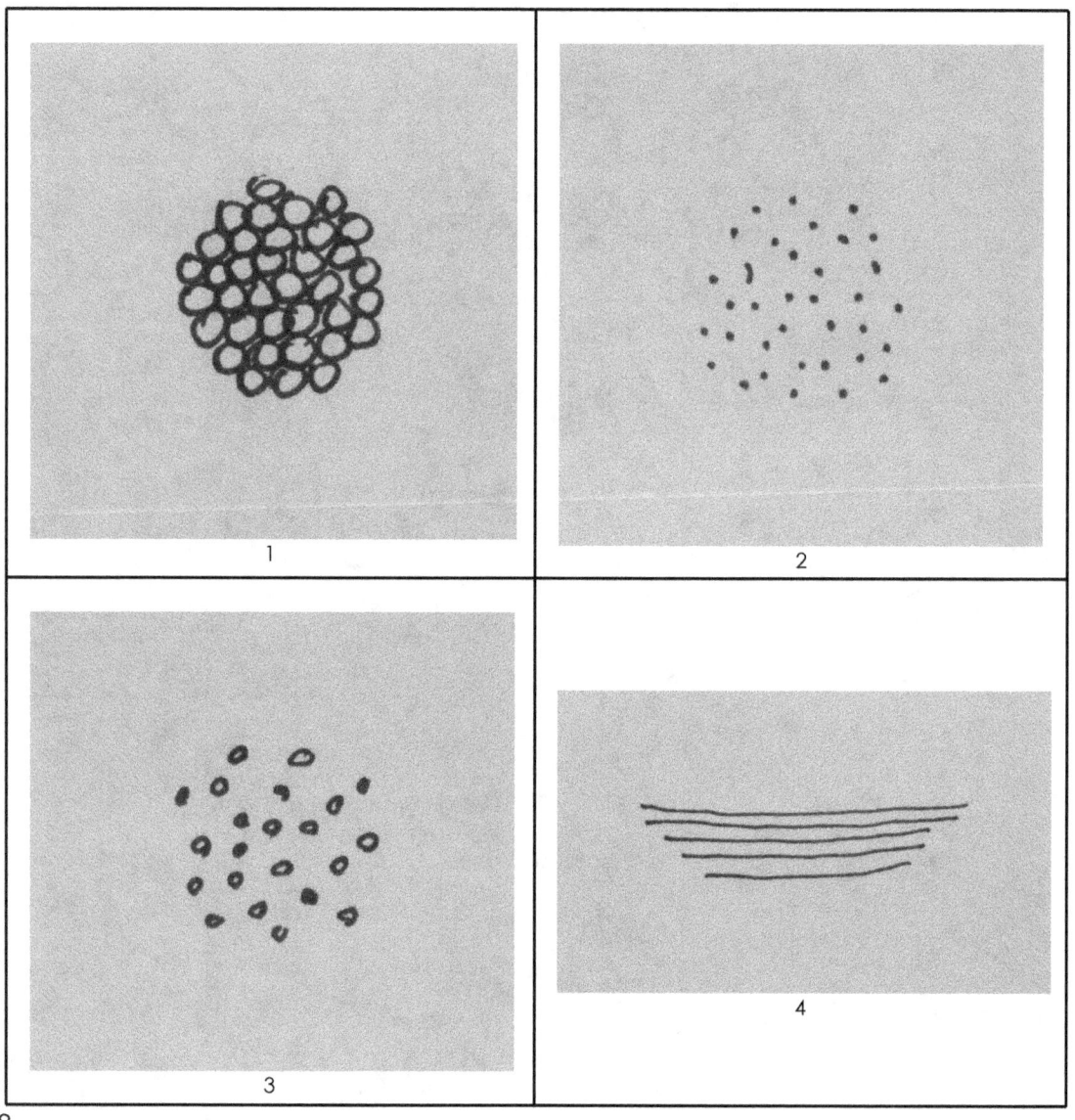

1

2

3

4

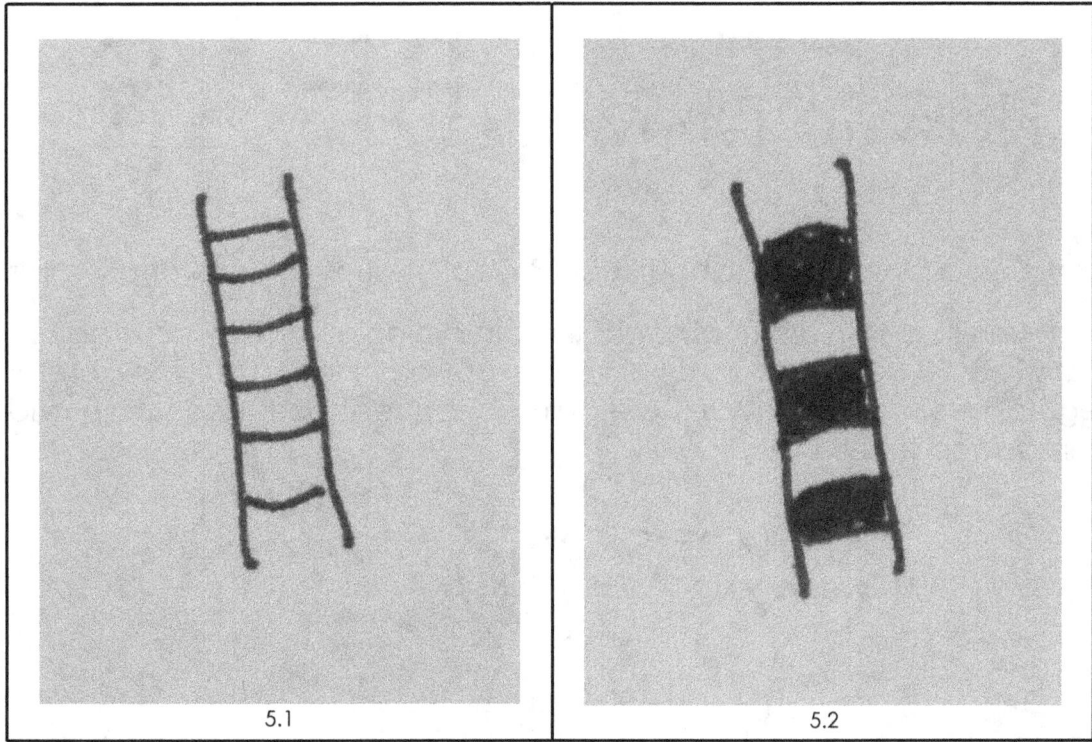

5.1   5.2

Your future Patterns gallery located in pages 31, 32 and 33. There, you can create many different repetitive patterns which you will use later in your drawings.

How to Draw a BEAR

What do you know about bear? Bear makes up a group that is related in its evolutionary descent from the miacid. Miacid is a creature that lived 50 million years ago. Bears are omnivores, but they prefer vegetable food. Omnivores are animals that eat both vegetable and animal food to survive.

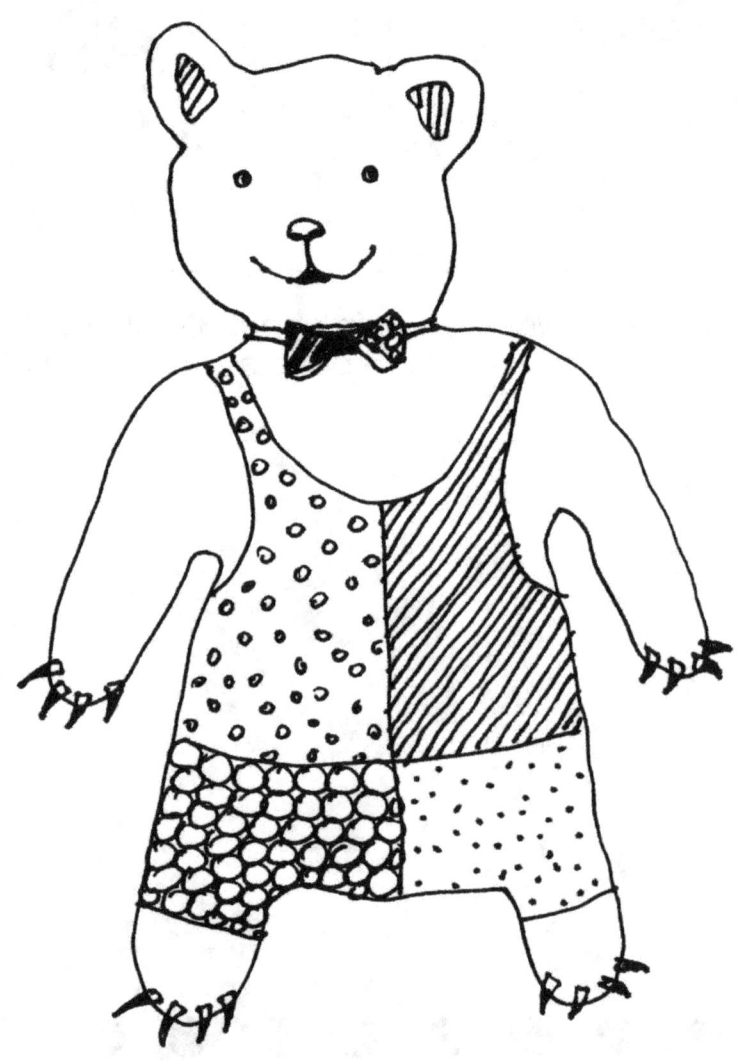

The bear may stand over 10 feet tall on its hind legs and weights more than 650 kilogram. The body weight depends on the family, and the males are generally heavier than the females. They tend to be long-furred, with most species colored, mainly brown or black. But there are also white Polar bears. They usually have 40 or 42 teeth depending upon species.

Bears tend to be good swimmers and climbers. They can maintain speeds of up to 50 km/hr. Some species hibernate during much of the winter season. They are relatively intelligent, resourceful animals with large, well-developed brains.

The following pages will show you how with ink pen step-by-step to draw bear. Every following image includes new details. Remember that you need no eraser. If a 'mistake' made, it will 'disappear' with the following repetitive patterns that will make your drawing beautiful and its composition balancing. The complete image will look like on the left.

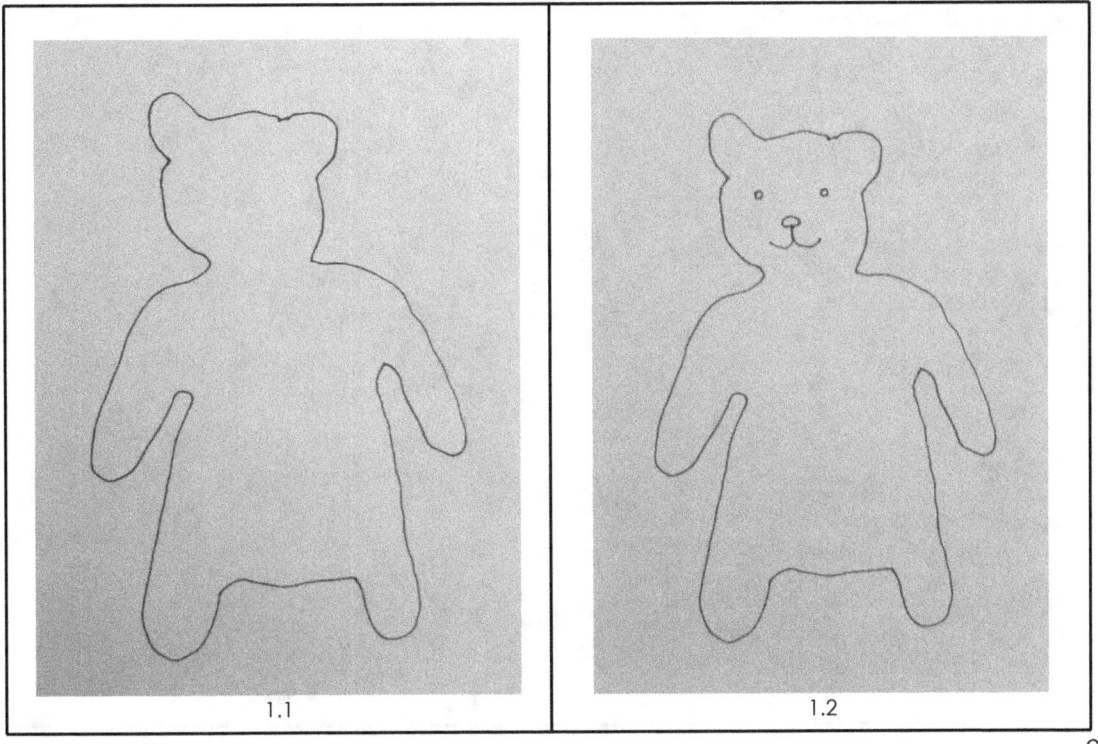

1.1 1.2

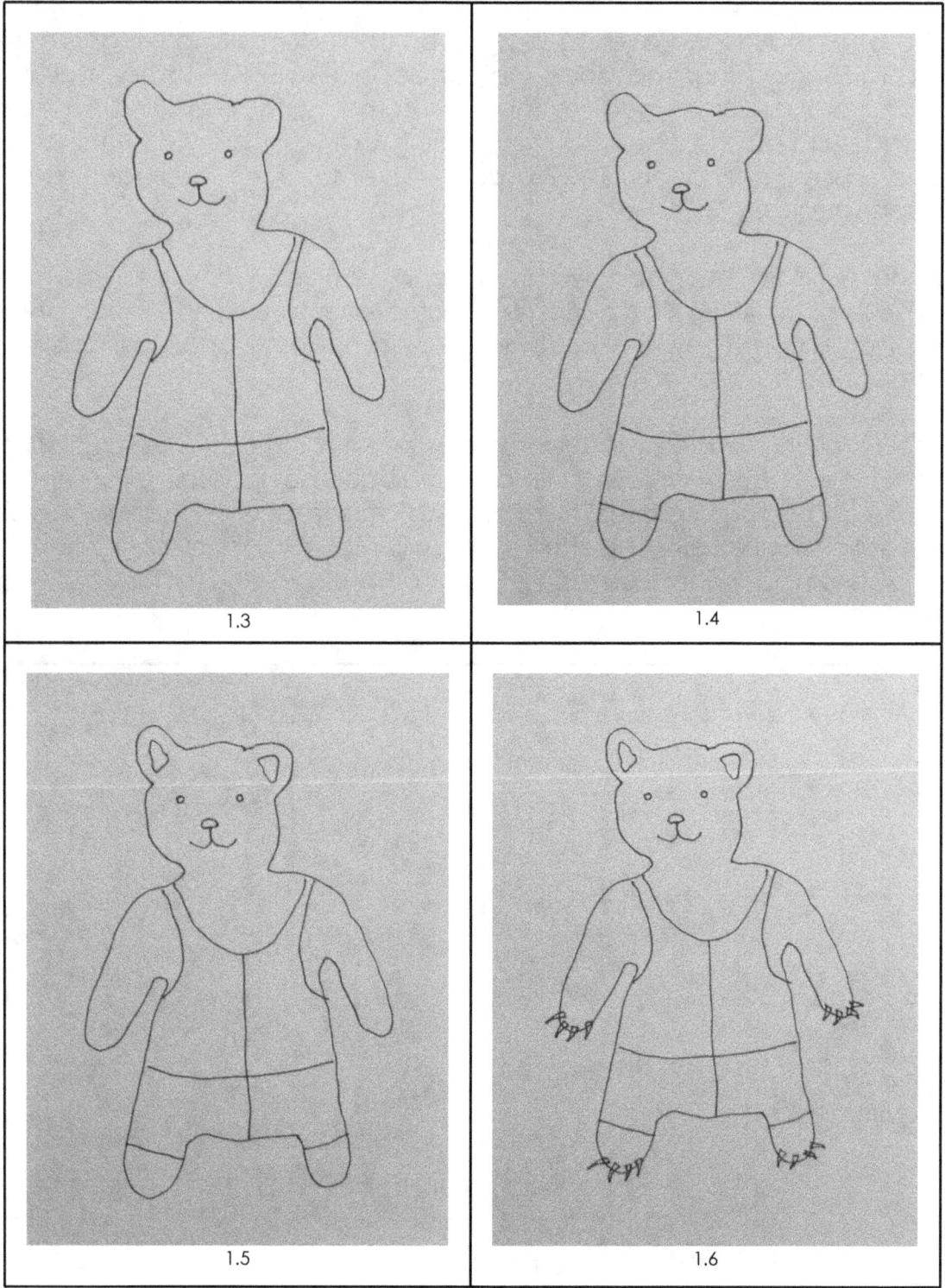

1.3

1.4

1.5

1.6

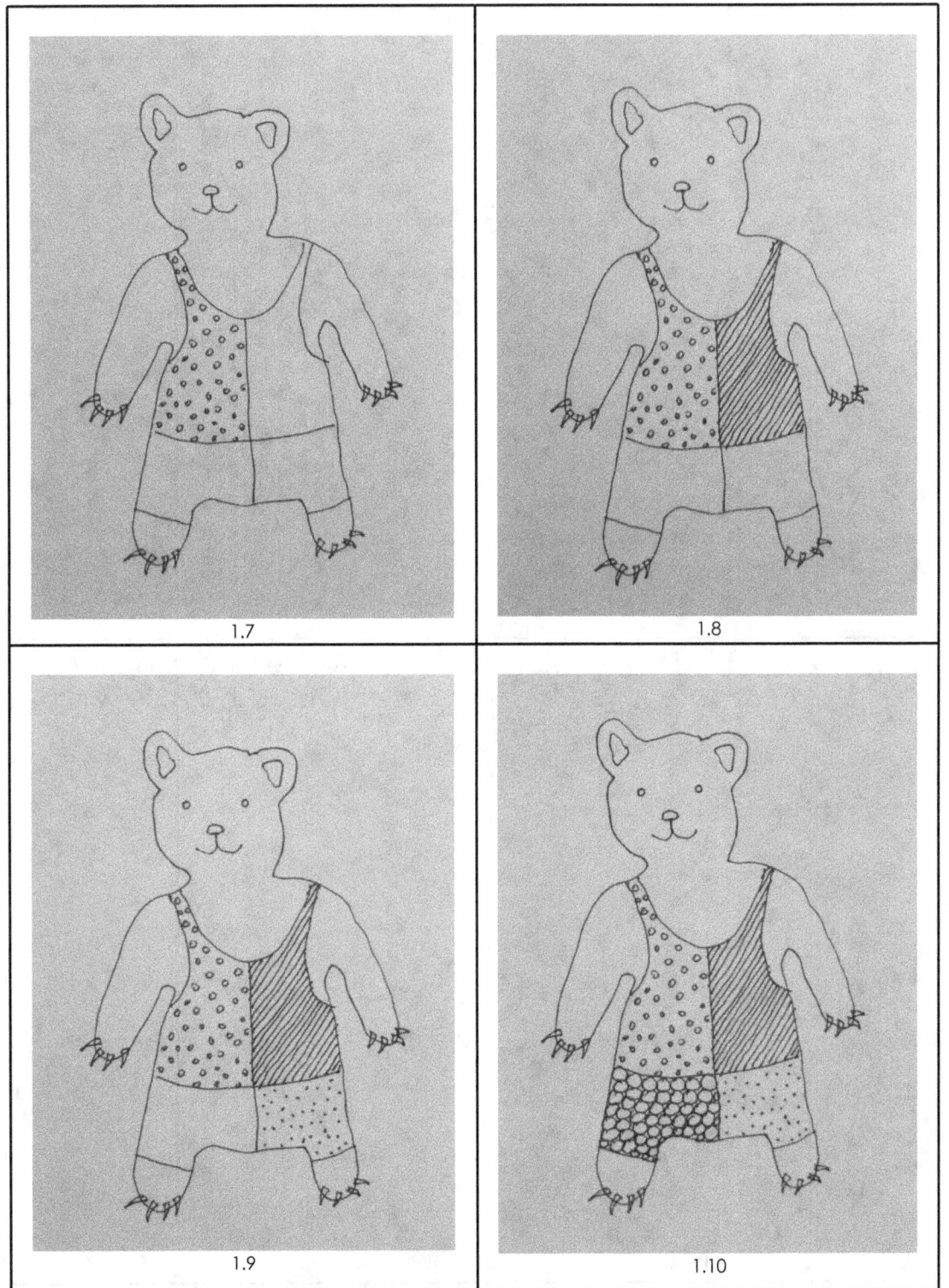

1.7

1.8

1.9

1.10

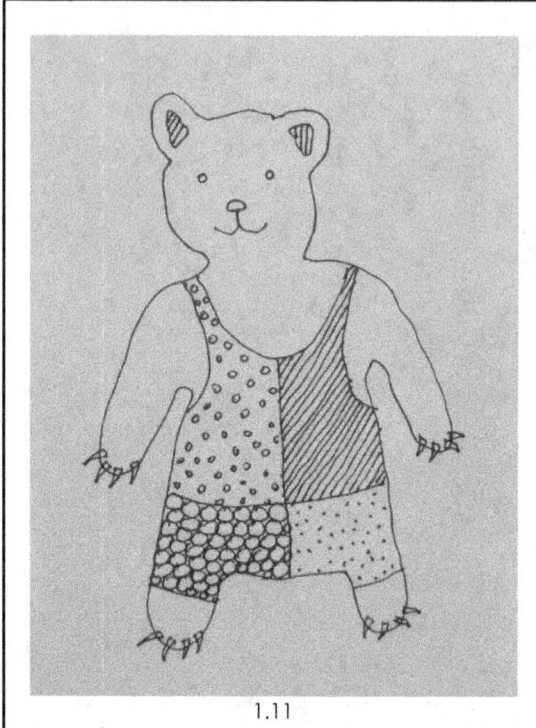

1.11

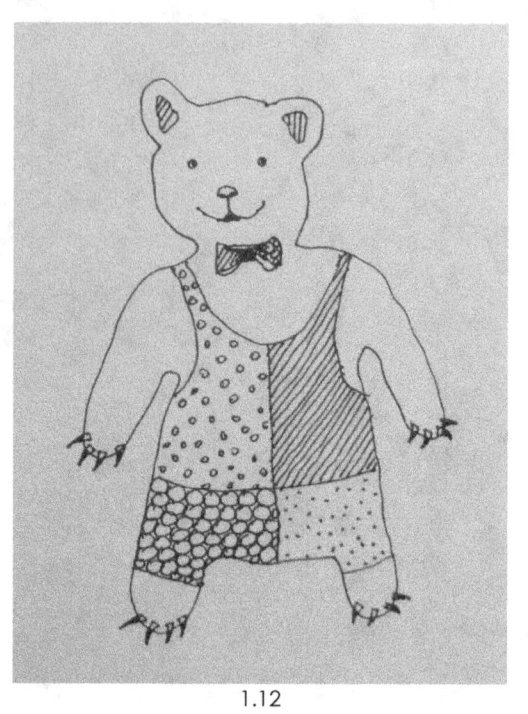

1.12

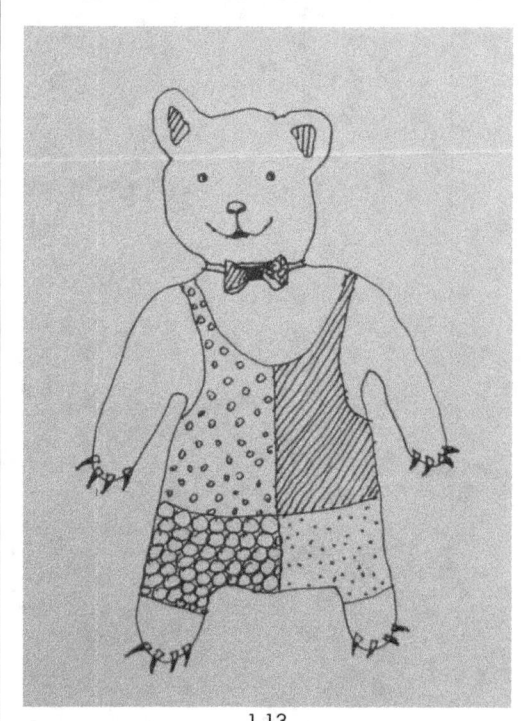

1.13

To see enlarged
patterns, used in this drawing,
visit pages
18, 19.

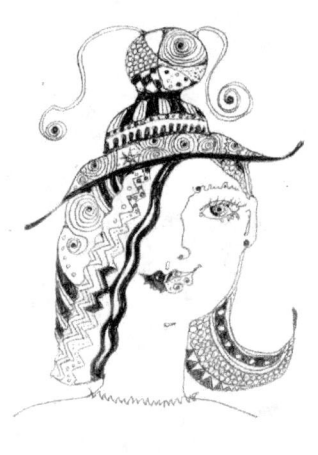

How to Draw a RABBIT

Rabbit is beautiful, kind and friendly. Rabbits hide their nests in plain view, often putting them in the open; for example, in the middle of the lawn. Rabbit mothers nurse their babies for approximately 5 minutes a day. They build a nest with grasses and fur to keep the babies warm in between feedings.

Rabbits can be from 20 cm (8 in) in length and 0.4 kg in weight to 50 cm (20 in) and more than 2 kg. Their fur is commonly long and soft, with colors such as shades of brown, gray, and buff. The tail is a little plume of brownish. Rabbits have ears that are long, narrow and erect. They are prey animals and are constantly aware of their surroundings. Rabbits are herbivores that feed by grazing on grass, forbs, and leafy weeds.

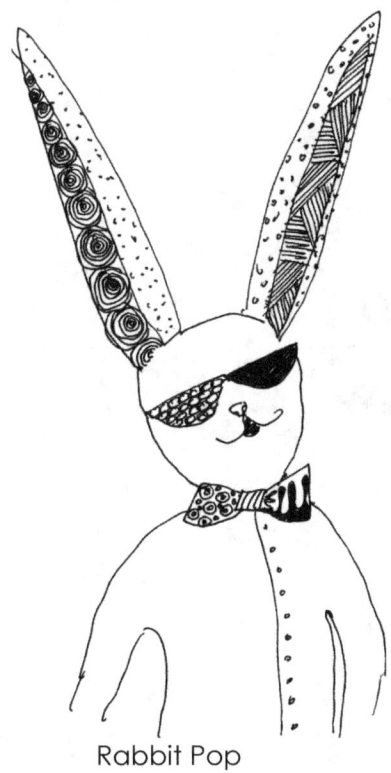

Rabbit Pop

The following pages will show you how with ink pen, step-by-step to draw a rabbit. Every following image includes new details. Remember, that you need no eraser. If you made a mistake, it will disappear with the following repetitive patterns that will make your drawing beautiful. The complete image will look like this:

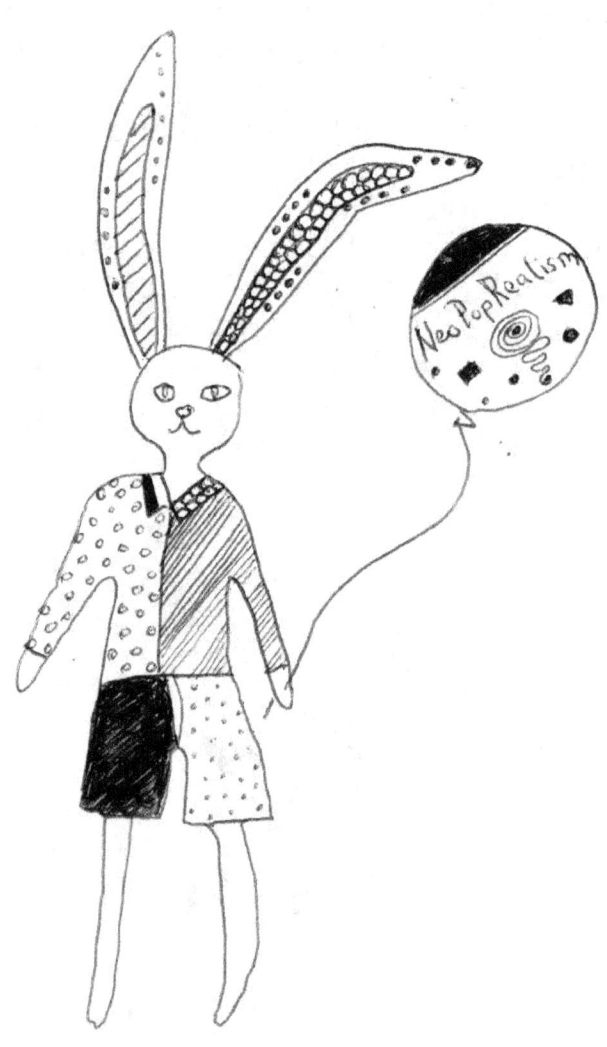

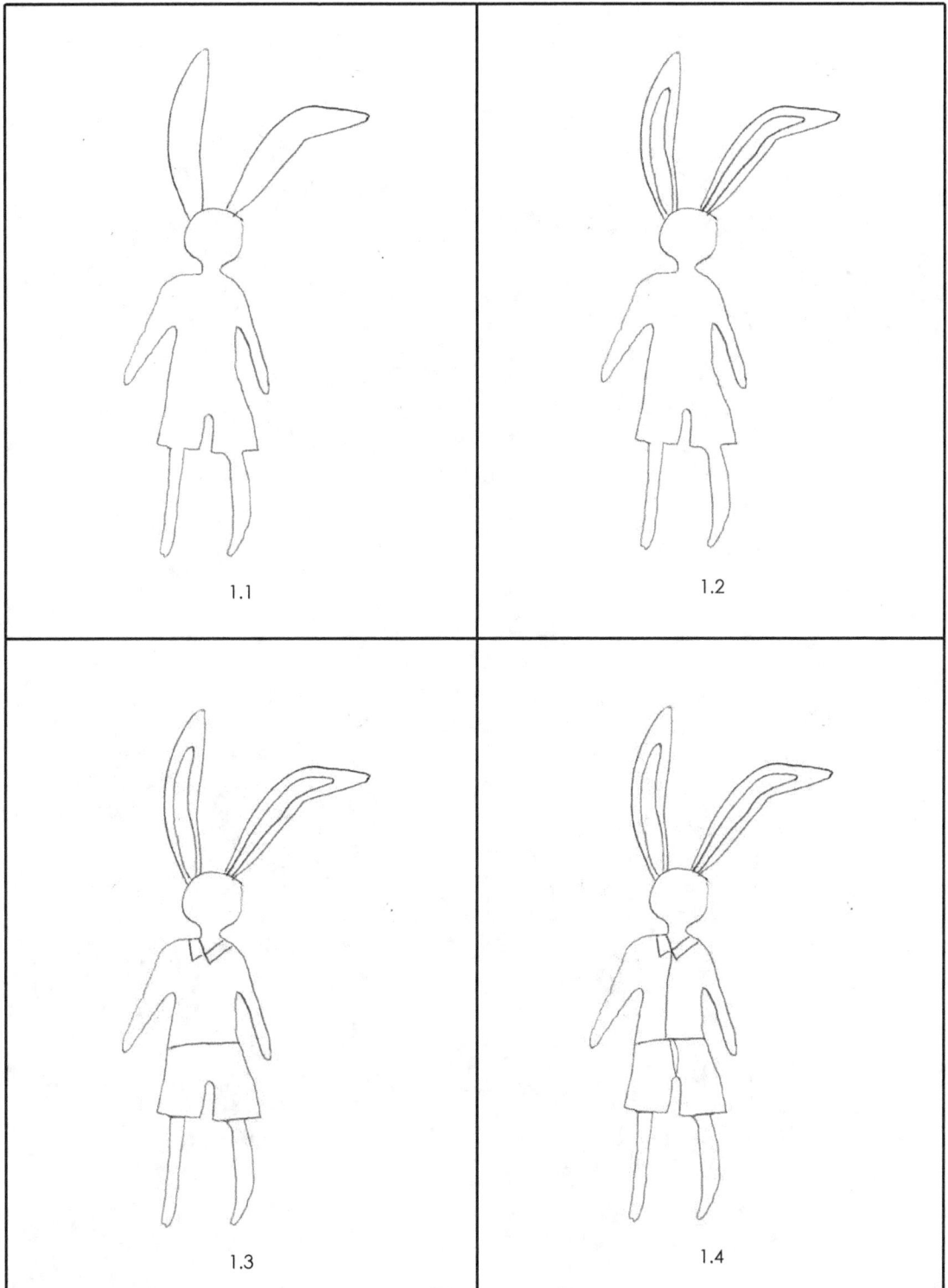

1.1

1.2

1.3

1.4

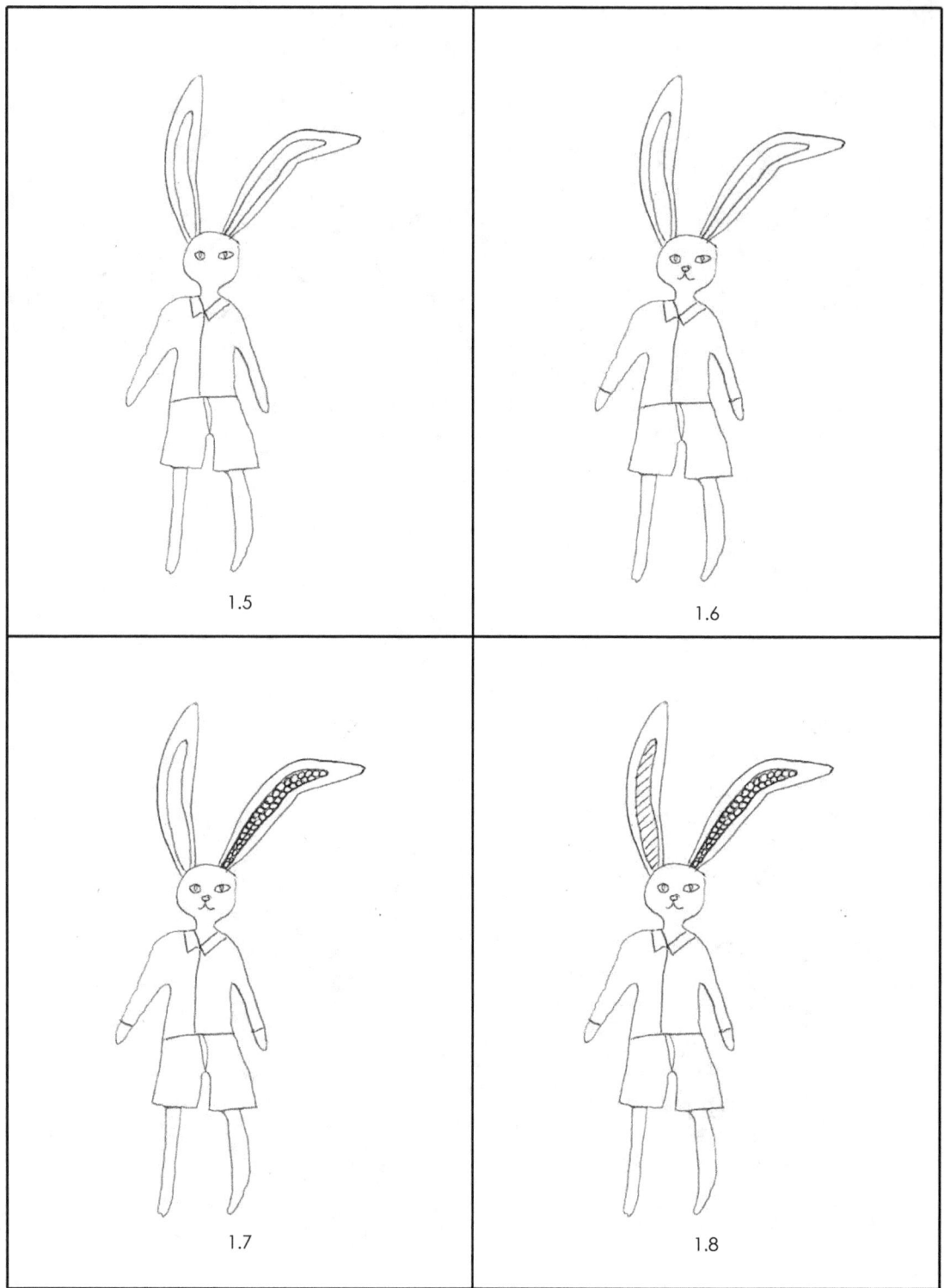

1.5

1.6

1.7

1.8

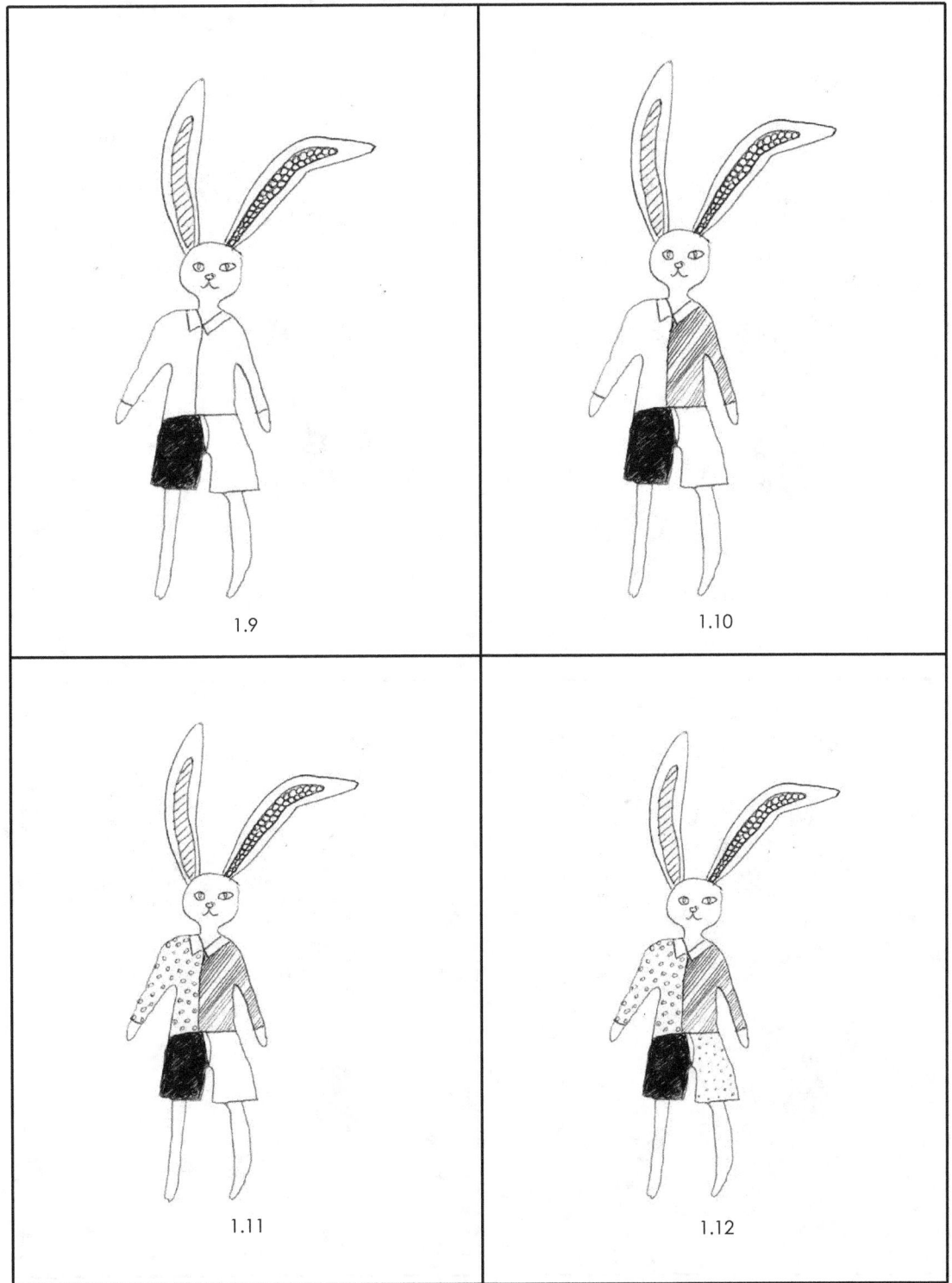

1.9

1.10

1.11

1.12

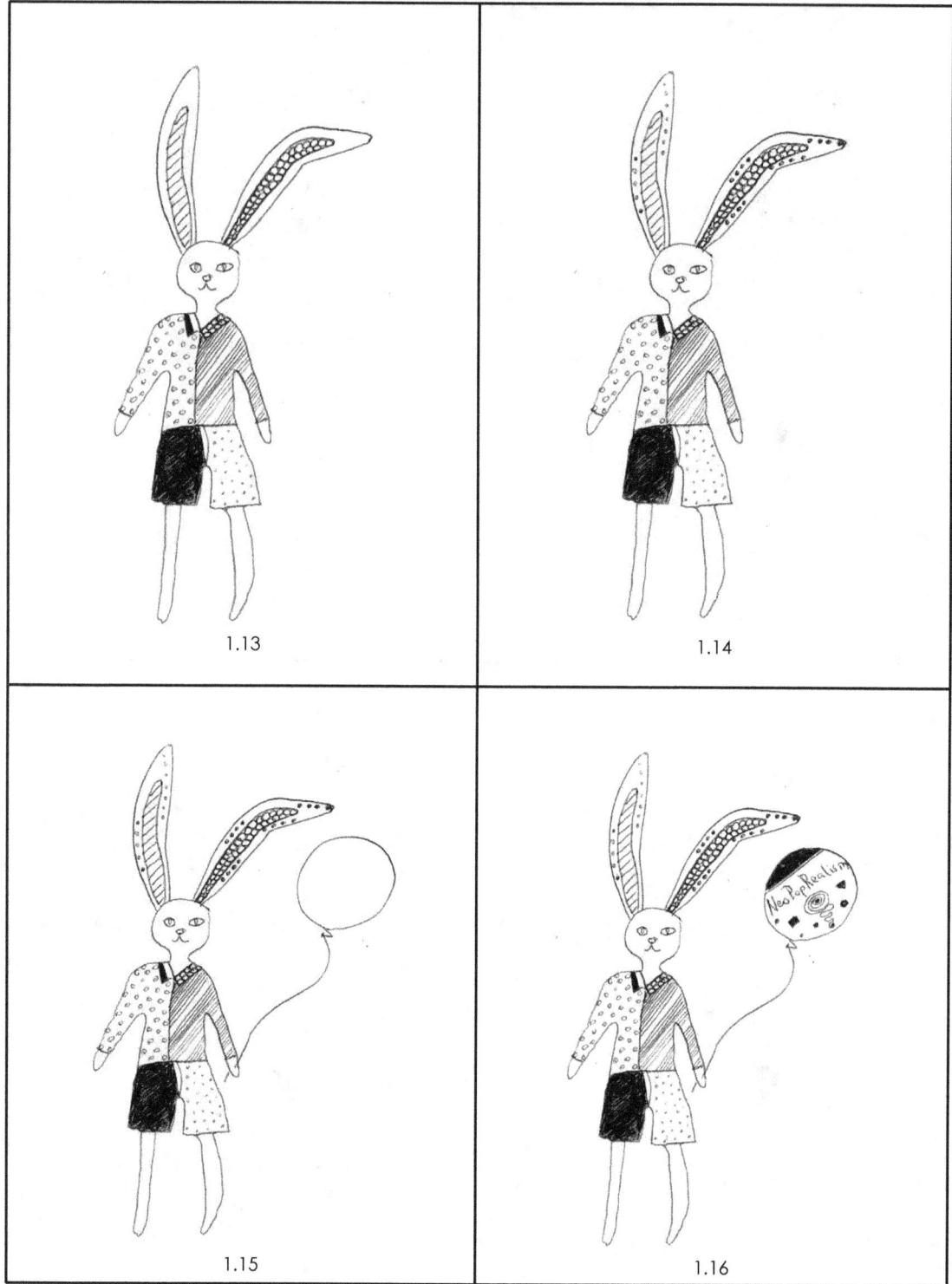

1.13

1.14

1.15

1.16

Your patterns gallery

The following pages are for you to draw the different repetitive patterns, which later you will use in your drawings. Create any patterns you wish, use zigzags, circles, triangles, squares, rectangular, lines dots, their combinations and variations. Be creative, develop your artistic skills!

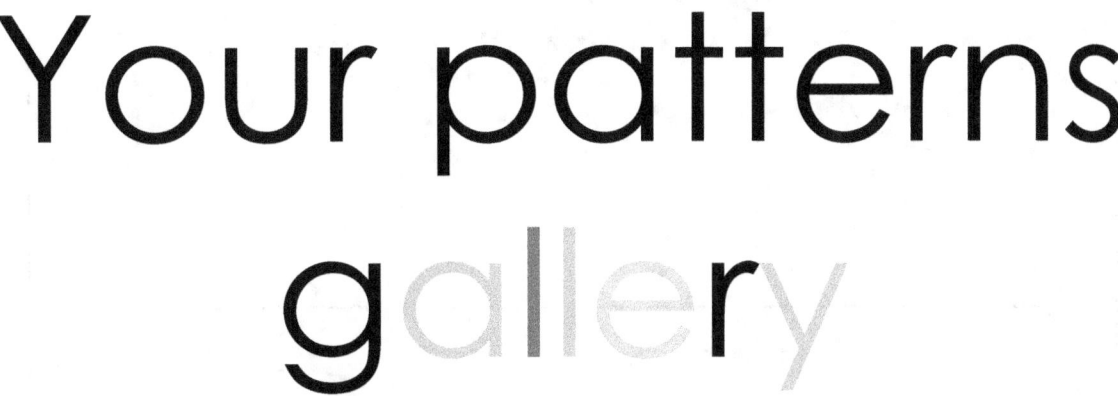 Neo: Let's get started!	1	2
3	4	5

6	7	8
9	10	11
12	13	14
15	16	17

18	19	20
21	22	23
24	25	26
27	28	29

Your exercising pages

These pages are for you to draw images here and now, from its beginning to the end, and to show what you have learned from this book. Follow all instructions and tips, some of them are below. No doubts, you will make some wonderful drawings. If not today, continue practicing, and you will learn how to draw any way.

Preparation:
~ Prepare ink pen.
~ Chose size of paper you like to use.
~ Decide what kind animal you would like to draw, person or may be flower... Do not copy them from the photographs, try to use your memory and your imagination.
~ If you do not remember how some details of the body look, only then you will need to have a photograph to look at it periodically.

The Process:
~ Use ink pen. Draw the contours of the animal's or person's body or flower, anyone or anything you wish to draw.
~ Continue to create with line the details of the animal's or person's body - eyes, nose, ears, clothes, etc.
~ Then, fill with *different* repetitive patterns some or all appeared sections. If you already created your *Repetitive patterns gallery* (pages 31, 32, 33), chose your patterns from there.

Enjoy the creative process, it is fun! Focus on what you are doing, and try to make it best you can. When you finish your drawing, relax! Then, draw another animal, person or flower, anything you wish. Play with line and repetitive patterns.

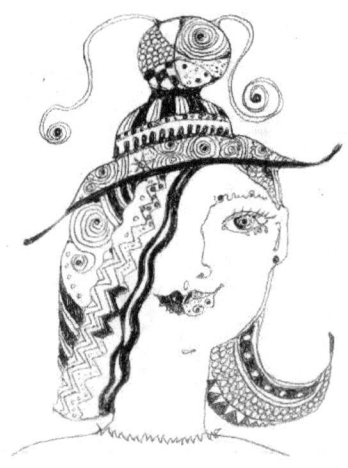

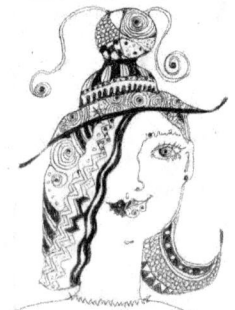

Neo:
Show to me
what you can do!

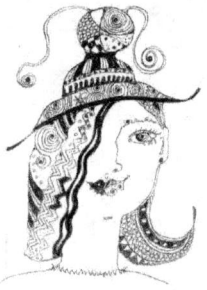

www.ingramcontent.com/pod-product-compliance
Lightning Source LLC
Chambersburg PA
CBHW081258180526
45170CB00007B/2483